ENCORE FOR CHOIRS 2

30 Crowd-pleasing Concert Pieces

Compiled by Peter Gritton

MUSIC DEPARTMENT

OXFORD

UNIVERSITY PRESS

OXFORD
UNIVERSITY PRESS

Great Clarendon Street, Oxford OX2 6DP, England
198 Madison Avenue, New York, NY10016, USA

Oxford University Press is a department of the University of Oxford.
It furthers the University's objective of excellence in research, scholarship,
and education by publishing worldwide

3 5 7 9 10 8 6 4

ISBN 10 0–19–343632–9
ISBN 13 978–0–19–343632–9

Music and text origination by
Enigma Music Engraving Ltd., Amersham, Bucks.
Printed in Great Britain on acid-free paper by
Biddles Ltd., King's Lynn, Norfolk

PREFACE

Encores for Choirs 2 follows hard on the heels of its predecessor owing to the ever-increasing demand for collections of short, effective pieces suitable for either thrilling or wooing an audience. There are 30 pieces contained in this volume, over half of which, while already very popular by some means, appear in print for the first time; in this way it is quite distinct from its sister volume in which a healthy number of pieces were already printed, established classics.

    Encores 2 has a particular cutting edge in the inclusion of items used by some of today's top *a cappella* vocal ensembles; as you read on you will discover who they are! Another important consideration in the thinking behind this volume was to include music from as many parts of the world as appropriately possible while still retaining a well-proportioned balance of material: hence about half a dozen pieces come from countries other than the States or UK—this figure *not* including the six adaptations of music by Bach, Handel, Mozart (2), Borodin, and Offenbach! There was still room to incorporate 18 pieces that find their origins in either the US or the UK—in fair proportion.

    This anthology would not be complete without two tunes that seem as old as the hills: firstly, **Shenandoah**, appearing here in the famous arrangement by James Erb which he wrote for the European tour made by the University Choir of Richmond (Virginia, US) way back in 1971. This version of the Virginian folksong is as magical as it ever was, and somehow manages to capture the enormity of the Missouri River within its rolling textures as well as the poet's obviously painful plight as he pines for his now distant valley of Shenando' (in Virginia). This is America's original river shanty, sung well over two hundred years ago by the likes of cavalrymen, some of whom had left home to marry Native Americans. Like 'Shenandoah', **Auld Lang Syne** is one of those ageless pentatonic folksongs; but unlike the former, its wordsmith is known—none other than the great Robert Burns. He penned this poem as an ode to friendship, the outstanding success of its sentiment being measured by the fact that 'Auld Lang Syne' is sung not just in Burns's native Scotland but by people all over the world. This is an undisputed Scottish classic, more commonly sung in unison/octaves by all and sundry, but here in a highly desirable arrangement by Joanna Forbes as used by the Swingle Singers, the internationally acclaimed eight-strong vocal group.

    Country Gardens is a traditional tune made famous by Percy Grainger (1882–1961) in his piano duet version published just after the First World War; this was an era when many British folksongs were preserved by the endeavours of Cecil Sharp. 'Country Gardens' was originally entitled 'Handkerchief Dance'—one in which traditional Morris dancers would involve some form of decorative handkerchief or neck-tie in their routine. Along with Sharp, composers such as Grainger and Vaughan Williams were anxious to preserve the folksong heritage of Britain which, together with local dialects, was dying out as the countryside became more and more threatened by industry. The mention of 'country' in Grainger's new title was therefore no accident. In this new arrangement, the tune is hidden to begin with but emerges by the end in its full splendour. **Dashing Away with the Smoothing Iron** is another folksong collected by Cecil Sharp and friends—in this instance from Somerset in South-west England. John Rutter's arrangement has the required lightness of touch and skilfully gives the tune to each voice at some point along the way. Part of the humour of this song is the farcical improbability that the whole clothes-washing process lasted from Monday to Saturday!

    Gustav Holst's rumbustious **Bring us in good ale** sounds like a folksong but is actually his own music to fifteenth-century words. Holst (1874–1934) was also from the folksong-collecting era and was most familiar with the modes and melodic shapes of traditional material. This song is nothing less than a raucous ode to alcohol. It is best sung when either still *just* sober, or the prospect of a visit to the ale-house is very strong! Like 'Bring us in good ale', John Rutter's **It was a lover and his lass** is an original setting of much older words —in this instance by William Shakespeare. Rutter wrote it for The Scholars (a group founded at the same time as the King's Singers while its members were at Cambridge University); it was first performed in 1975 and is still as popular as ever.

Deconstructing Johann is the King's Singers' wonderful offering to this anthology and the witty work of Daryl Runswick—one of their favourite arrangers. This piece is less of an arrangement, more of a composition, in the sense that Runswick has not only formed the most amazing collage of J. S. Bach's 'greatest hits' but written his own lyrics to create an extraordinary scenario. **Three-minute Messiah** runs along similar lines in that it is a collage, but has been created especially for *Encores 2* for quite different reasons: Handel's renowned oratorio *Messiah* tells the great Christian story in a musical drama lasting for well over two hours. 'Three-minute Messiah' tells the same story but 'in the twinkling of an eye'—perfect if you don't have time to sing the whole oratorio as an encore!

Stranger in Paradise has one of the musical world's best-loved melodies and is the result of Wright and Forrest's idea to create *Kismet* (1953)—a Broadway musical based on the Russian composer Borodin's opera *Prince Igor* (1888), using his music but adding a new storyline. Wright and Forrest used a melody from the opera's Polovetzian Dances for what was to become the hit song from their musical, probably responsible alone for the musical being turned into a movie after only a few years. **Ill Wind (I once had a horn)** is the transformation of the finale of Mozart's Fourth Horn Concerto to create a quite different effect altogether: Flanders and Swann was a British double act at its prime in the 1950s and '60s delivering revues on both sides of the Atlantic. In one of these shows, Michael Flanders (pretending that he played the French horn) introduced the duo's version of Mozart's famous rondo with the following words: 'I had hoped this evening to give you the very first performance of the last movement, the Rondo Allegro Vivace. Owing to curious circumstances as yet unexplained I am not able to do this. I can only tell you why . . .'.

Three other items in *Encores 2* are concoctions of musical masterpieces with new, zappy words. I am delighted to be able to include one of Cantabile's showstoppers **Orpheus in the Underground**: Cantabile—a four-man vocal outfit based in the UK but renowned in many countries across the globe—take us on their hilarious journey in the London Underground. The can-can from Offenbach's *Orpheus in the Underworld* seems ideally suited to such an adventure, and if you dig out your London tube map, it all makes perfect sense! The lyrics are by the brilliant John Hudson who originally wrote this for the Cambridge Footlights. **Take it from Figure 'O'** is the brainchild of ex-Swingle Ben Parry who has cunningly devised a guided tour to the musical elements of Mozart's operatic overture to *The Marriage of Figaro* with added comic patter; also prevalent is melodramatic tension between 'characters'—basses complaining, tenors showing off, sopranos and altos often moaning about their male counter-parts . . . but all beaten into submission—thus united—by Mozart's emphatic, repetitious final cadences. **'Un'-Popular Song** is a witty adaptation of the famous tap-dance from Walton's cabaret entertainment *Façade*. Robin Barry and Roddy Williams have created a most subtle *tour de force* for any choir or mixed barbershop group—every minute of careful rehearsal worth it!

There comes a point when music can touch those parts of us that words just cannot reach: Rachmaninov's **Vocalise** is one such piece. He originally wrote it as the conclusion to a sequence of 14 songs for soprano and piano, its lack of words having exactly the aforementioned effect. Owing to the popularity of 'Vocalise' in itself, it has been performed as a single piece by soprano with orchestral accompaniment and on most instruments with piano accompaniment. 'Vocalise' lends itself beautifully to the choral medium, with each voice-part heavily in the melodic action. In complete contrast, Jaakko Mäntyjärvi's quirky **El Hambo** relies almost entirely on the delivery of the words which, ironically, mean absolutely nothing! The *hambo* is a traditional Swedish dance in three-time: Mäntyjärvi distorts the metre, often cranking it into 5/4 which, in the composer's own words, 'is something of a tribute to those folk musicians whose enthusiasm much exceeds their sense of rhythm'. Even the Swedish chef on *The Muppet Show* was inspiration to the composer in this barnstormer. As for **Chick, chick, chicken!**, this is sheer silliness in a nutshell—or perhaps one should say eggshell. First heard as sung by Tom Stacks with Harry Reser's '6 Jumping Jacks' in 1926, Holt, McGhee, and King's crazy song has long attained nursery-rhyme status all round the world—a tribute to its extraordinary genius.

There are ten original compositions in this volume: **Jargon** was written by William Billings (1746–1800), arguably the first great American composer. Here dissonance represents his abhorrence of the British occupation of his home town Boston, Massachusetts, in 1775–6. The piece served as a defiant conclusion to his anthem *Lamentation over Boston*. Sounding more like a twentieth-century work, 'Jargon' has the most extraordinary impact, particularly when sung at full volume. **Parting Friends** is another piece from America's past which, with its sparse fourths and fifths, is an ancestor to the ilk of Aaron Copland and modern-day Hollywood film composers—arranged in this manner by John McCurry in the 1870s. This is a folksong that encapsulates eighteenth- and nineteenth-century American adventurism and its obvious dangers as peoples gradually migrated across the continent, leaving loved ones behind. At the other extreme, the all-American folksong **Buffalo Gals** is designed to rock the rafters in this new arrangement by the increasingly popular Bob Chilcott. The sound of a fiddle is subtly woven into the texture as the guys and gals get it together in a rumbustious dance. Chilcott's other contribution to this anthology is another boisterous one: the spiritual **Ev'ry time I feel the Spirit** is set in joyous mood. This song is more commonly sung quietly and meditatively but works equally well in upbeat fashion, especially as it picks up on the reference in the last verse to that new (in those days) invention—the steam train—and propels us on the one-way track to heaven. Interestingly, 'Underground Railroad' was the name given to the organization that helped slaves escape in the nineteenth century. Also, Ohio River was sometimes referred to as 'Jordan River', beyond which lay potential freedom for slaves. As you would imagine, the text of this spiritual may have hidden messages, some long forgotten.

The other spiritual in *Encores 2*, **Dry Bones**, conjures up African roots with its powerful yet playful text. The original melody is unbelievably simple in its formation from just a handful of notes. It is based on the vision of the Old Testament prophet Ezekiel, in which he witnesses a desert of human bones coming back to life. For the slaves, this image of rebirth would have instilled hope and a sense of unity against all their afflictions; these days, it stands as a song of great joy, genuinely released from its troubled past. **Good Hope** is an original composition, using a concoction of African texts and drawing on various musical styles from the continent. At the start (bars 1–29), the tenors and basses sing in Ethiopian while the sopranos and altos sing in Xhosa (South Africa)—the meaning of this revealed in the English words sung at the very end. The initial joyous mood is momentarily interrupted by an ominous drum roll, the Nigerian text at this point telling us not to look back at past troubles (therefore forwards to a new future), after which the piece breaks into joyous mood once again. The use of several African languages is a symbol of hope for peace and unity.

Wiegenlied, by Johannes Brahms (1832–97), now has folksong status bestowed upon it. Significantly, Brahms wrote to Clara Schumann: 'Songs today have gone so far astray that one cannot cling too closely to one's ideal, and that ideal is folksong'. The title literally means 'cradle song' (or 'lullaby') and was written as one of five songs for solo voice and piano in 1868. This arrangement was made recently for members of the Berlin Radio Choir. **Nachtlied** is one of those rare jewels that adorn the choral repertoire. Max Reger (1873–1916) was a most versatile musician—composer, pianist, organist, conductor, and professor. This 'song of the night', a setting of a poem by Petrus Herbert (1591), was written only two years before Reger's premature death and covers the whole gamut of expression. **Calme des nuits**, another nocturne-like gem, was written in 1882 by Camille Saint-Saëns (1835–1921). He was also a musician of diverse ability—composer, pianist, organist, and teacher—and wrote this miniature masterpiece after several troubled years during which he lost two children and then separated from his wife. Like the Reger, it covers a great timbral range in a short space of time.

Interestingly, Saint-Saëns was the first recognized composer to write for film (in 1908), a genre that has since inspired many a fine score. The music for **Mission: Impossible** is one such example of a modern-day classic with its pulsating irregular metre. This volume would not be complete without Lalo Schifrin's theme tune, arranged by Mark Williams for the Swingle Singers and here specially adapted by him for *Encores 2* to suit a four-part choir.

Sir Arthur Sullivan's unwitting contribution of two items to *Encores 2* shows that even a century after his death his popularity remains intact. **The Long Day Closes** is a sublime partsong, originally written for men's voices (in D major) in 1868. While the poet summons up an image of self-pity, Sullivan is really in his element here, managing to lift the subject's state on to quite another level with his spellbinding harmony. He was the master of the miniature and, of course, the operetta: **A Modern Major-General** comes from *The Pirates of Penzance* (1879) and is an arrangement of Major-General Stanley's patter-song in which he boasts of his wide learning. The irony is that he was a bit of a buffoon and fools nobody but himself with such banter. This is possibly the most famous patter-song of all time. Sullivan's partnership with W. S. Gilbert resulted in 14 operettas spanning the last 30 or so years of the Victorian era, the majority of which, believe it or not, are still performed regularly.

The delightful **Counting Up My Toes** is on a par with 'Christopher Robin is saying his prayers' (*Encores 1*), the difference being that the former is a mock-Edwardian piece written by a contemporary composer, David Cullen. It is a particular favourite of the four-man group Cantabile, who woo their audiences worldwide with this cutesy number! At the other extreme, if you wish to leave your listeners feeling philosophical, try Howard Skempton's brand new **The tide rises, the tide falls**. Skempton is a British composer with a distinctive compositional voice, at his most individual in this setting of Longfellow's eerie poem.

What makes a good 'encore'? This is a hard question to answer since each concert is a unique moment in itself and there can be no prescribed formula. However, we hope that within this anthology there is sufficient variety—from the classic to the cutting-edge—to keep you satisfied, at least for the time being!

PETER GRITTON

Acknowledgements

I am particularly grateful to the members of the three British-based groups Cantabile, the King's Singers, and the Swingle Singers for allowing us to publish some of their favourite party-pieces. Further details of these illustrious ensembles are available at

www.cantabile.com
www.kingssingers.com
www.swinglesingers.com

Philip Blackburn, Professor of Music at the University of Minnesota, was as helpful as he could possibly be in some research on William Billings. Many thanks to Mark Forkgen and his talented London-based choir Canticum who, together, test-ran a few items before publication. I am indebted to my editor (and lyricist!) at OUP, Robin Barry, who masterminded this project from its beginning with thoroughness and good humour. Finally, I wish to thank my wife Harriet for her patience, understanding, and cups of camomile tea.

P.W.G.

Compiler and General Editor

Peter Gritton studied music at Clare College, Cambridge before taking up a post at Christ Church, Oxford as a countertenor Lay Clerk. Peter has sung with a variety of groups, including The Sixteen, The Cambridge Singers, Gabrieli Consort, I Fagiolini, and a close harmony group, The Light Blues, with whom he has travelled worldwide. He currently teaches at St Paul's School, London, as well as enjoying a busy schedule composing, arranging, and singing.

Peter has had arrangements commissioned by the King's Singers. His music is published widely, including some arrangements in the close harmony anthology *In the Mood* and two carols, *Away in a manger* (composed on a new tune) and *Run with torches*, all available from Oxford University Press. He is also the compiler and editor of *Encores for Choirs 1*.

CONTENTS

page

1. **A Modern Major-General** Arthur Sullivan *arr.* Peter Gritton   1
2. **Auld Lang Syne** Scottish trad. *arr.* Joanna Forbes   12
3. **Bring us in good ale** Gustav Holst   20
4. **Buffalo Gals** American trad. *arr.* Bob Chilcott   25
5. **Calme des nuits** Camille Saint-Saëns   34
6. **Chick, chick, chicken!** Holt, McGhee, and King *arr.* Peter Gritton   37
7. **Counting Up My Toes** David Cullen   44
8. **Country Gardens** English trad. *arr.* Peter Gritton   47
9. **Dashing Away with the Smoothing Iron**   53
   English trad. *arr.* John Rutter
10. **Deconstructing Johann** Daryl Runswick   68
11. **Dry Bones** Spiritual *arr.* Peter Gritton   81
12. **El Hambo** Jaakko Mäntyjärvi   89
13. **Ev'ry time I feel the Spirit** Spiritual *arr.* Bob Chilcott   104
14. **Good Hope** Peter Gritton   113
15. **Ill Wind** Flanders and Swann after Mozart *arr.* Peter Gritton   118
16. **It was a lover and his lass** John Rutter   134
17. **Jargon** William Billings   143
18. **Mission: Impossible** Lalo Schifrin *arr.* Mark Williams   144
19. **Nachtlied** Max Reger   157
20. **Orpheus in the Underground** Jacques Offenbach *arr.* Cantabile   161
21. **Parting Friends** North American trad. *arr.* John G. McCurry   169
22. **Shenandoah** American trad. *arr.* James Erb   170
23. **Stranger in Paradise**   175
   Wright and Forrest after Borodin *arr.* Peter Gritton
24. **Take it from Figure 'O'** W. A. Mozart *arr.* Ben Parry   183
25. **The Long Day Closes** Arthur Sullivan   203
26. **The tide rises, the tide falls** Howard Skempton   206
27. **Three-minute Messiah** Peter Gritton   208
28. **'Un'-Popular Song** William Walton *arr.* Roderick Williams   218
29. **Vocalise** Sergei Rachmaninov *arr.* Peter Gritton   232
30. **Wiegenlied** Johannes Brahms *arr.* Robin Gritton   240

1. A Modern Major-General

W. S. Gilbert

ARTHUR SULLIVAN
arr. PETER GRITTON

Printed in Great Britain

OXFORD UNIVERSITY PRESS, MUSIC DEPARTMENT, GREAT CLARENDON STREET, OXFORD OX2 6DP

*The breath marks from bar 18 are optional dramatic pauses. They may or may not be taken to affect the tempo.

ve - ry well ac - quain - ted too with mat - ters ma - the - ma - ti - cal,
tell un - doubt - ed Ra - pha - els from Ge - rard Dows and Zoff - an - ies,

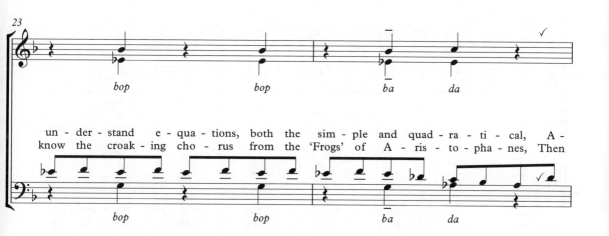

un - der - stand e - qua - tions, both the sim - ple and quad - ra - ti - cal, A -
know the croak - ing cho - rus from the 'Frogs' of A - ris - to - pha - nes, Then

a tempo

(spoken) lot o' news!
din a - fore!
pp

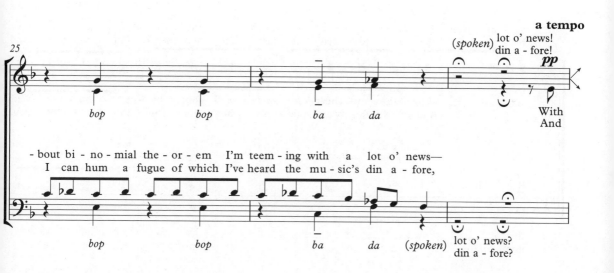

With
And

- bout bi - no - mial the - or - em I'm teem - ing with a lot o' news—
I can hum a fugue of which I've heard the mu - sic's din a - fore,

(spoken) lot o' news?
din a - fore?

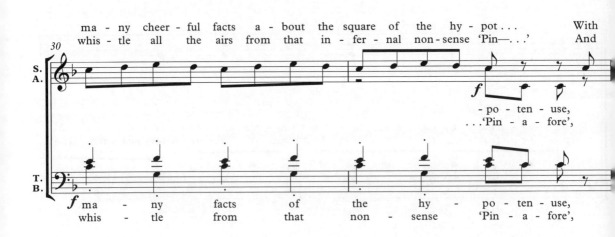

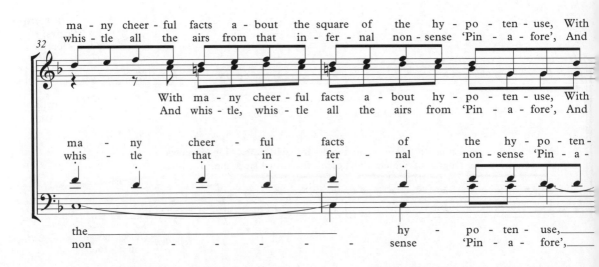

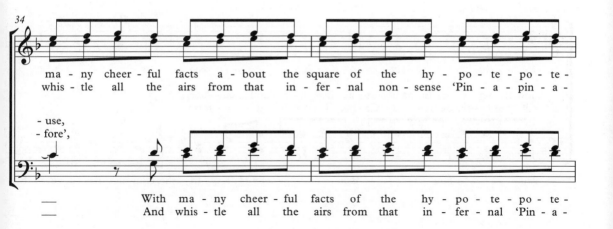

ma - ny cheer - ful facts a - bout the square of the hy - po - te - po - te -
whis - tle all the airs from that in - fer - nal non - sense 'Pin - a - pin - a -

- use,
- fore',

—
—

With ma - ny cheer - ful facts of the hy - te - po - te -
And whis - tle all the airs from that in - fer - nal 'Pin - a -

- nuse.
- fore'.

- nuse.
- fore'.

bap bap ba da bap bap ba ba ba ba ba

I'm
Then

- nuse.
- fore'.

mf

- nuse.
- fore'.

bap bap ba da bap bap ba ba ba ba ba ba ba ba

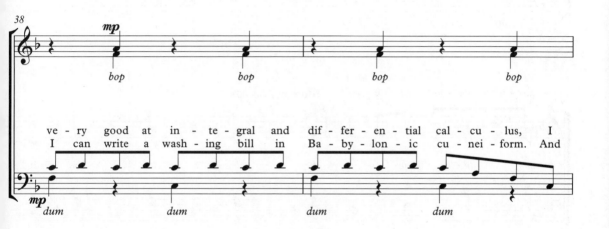

mp

bop bop bop bop

ve - ry good at in - te - gral and dif - fer - en - tial cal - cu - lus, I
I can write a wash - ing bill in Ba - by - lon - ic cu - nei - form. And

mp
dum dum dum dum

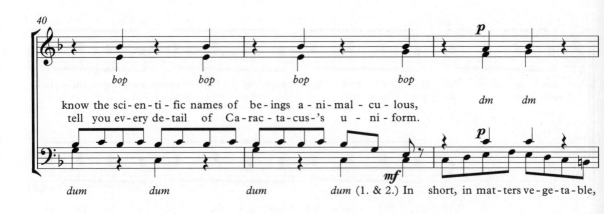

know the sci-en-ti-fic names of be-ings a-ni-mal-cu-lous,
tell you ev-ery de-tail of Ca-rac-ta-cus's u-ni-form.

a-ni-mal, and mi-ne-ral, I am the ve-ry mo-del of a mo-dern Ma-jor-Ge-ne-ral.

short, in mat-ters ve-ge-ta-ble, a-ni-mal, and mi-ne-ral, He is the ve-ry mo-del of a

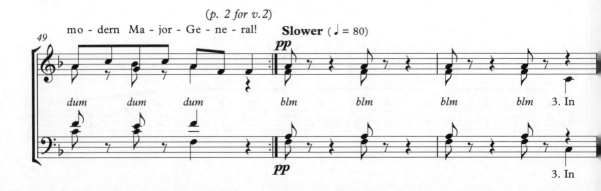

(p. 2 for v.2)

poco stringendo

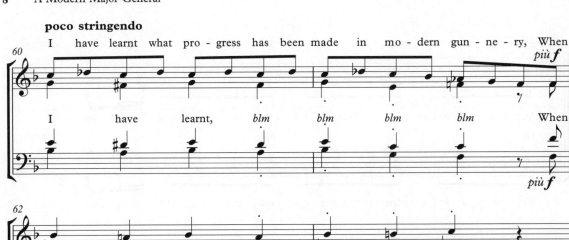

I have learnt what pro - gress has been made in mo - dern gun - ne - ry, When

piùf

I have learnt, *blm* *blm* *blm* *blm* When

piùf

I know more, *blm* *blm* *blm* *blm*

f I know more of tac - tics than a no - vice in a nun - ne - ry,

I know more, *blm* *blm* *blm* *blm* *p* In

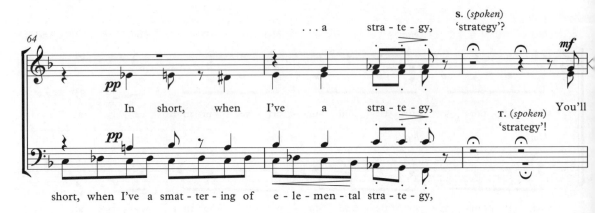

. . . a stra - te - gy, s. (*spoken*) 'strategy'? *mf*

pp

In short, when I've a stra - te - gy, t. (*spoken*) 'strategy'! You'll

pp

short, when I've a smat - ter - ing of e - le - men - tal stra - te - gy,

Vivace

S. say a bet - ter Ma - jor - Ge - ne - *ral* has ne - ver *sat* a gee—

A. say a bet - ter Ma - jor - Ge - ne - *ral* has ne - ver *sat* a gee—

You'll say a bet - ter Ma - jor - Ge - ne-

T.
B. *mf* dum   da   dum

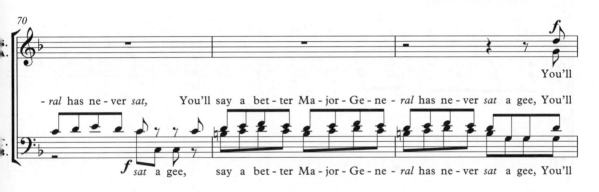

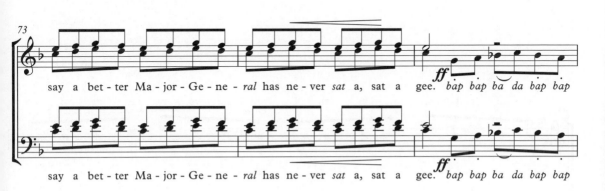

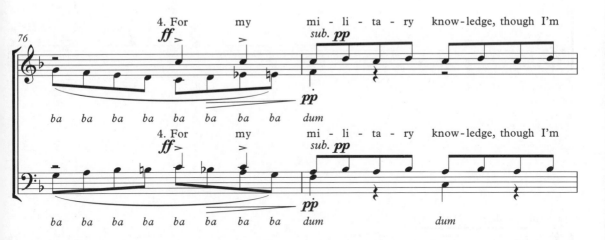

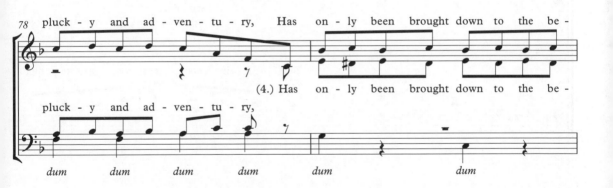

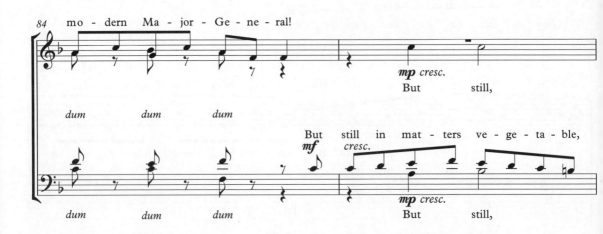

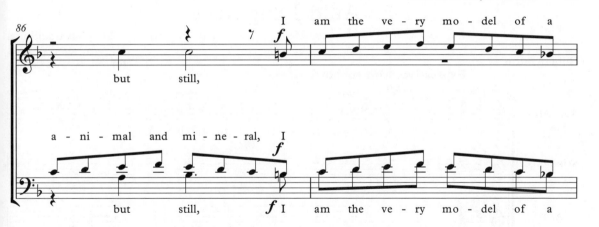

2. Auld Lang Syne

Scottish traditional
arr. JOANNA FORBES
for THE SWINGLE SINGERS

Robert Burns

Expressive, with rubato (♩ = 65)

The original version for eight-part choir is available from The Swingle Singers. **info@swinglesingers.com**

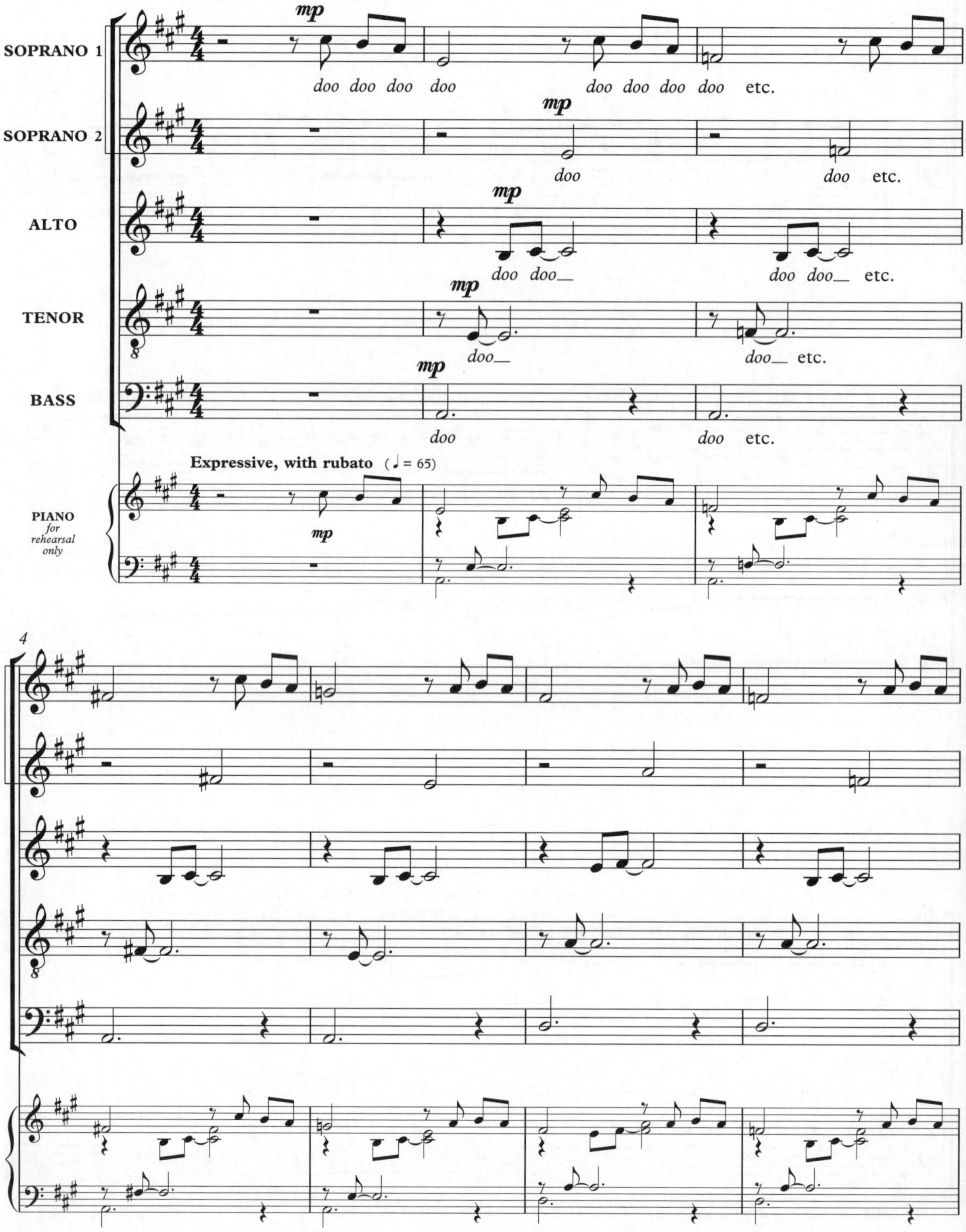

TENOR SOLO *mf*

Should auld ac-quain-tance be for-got, And
(old)

ne - ver brought to min'? Should auld ac-quain-tance be for-got, And
(mind)

S. thine;   We'll tak a cup o' kind - ness yet, for the sake of auld lang

A. thine;   We'll tak a cup o' kind - ness yet, for the sake of auld lang

T. thine;   We'll tak a cup o' kind - ness yet, for the sake of auld lang

B. thine;   We'll tak a cup o' kind - ness yet, for the sake of auld lang

syne.   For auld___ lang___ syne, my dear, for auld___ lang___

syne.   For auld___ lang___ syne, my dear, for auld___ lang

syne.   For auld lang___ syne, my dear, for auld___ lang

syne.   For auld___ lang___ syne, my dear, for auld lang

to Conrad Noel

3. Bring us in good ale

15th century

GUSTAV HOLST

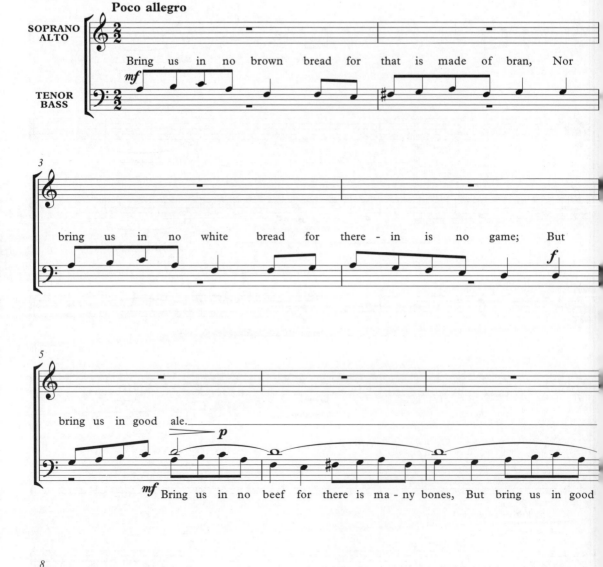

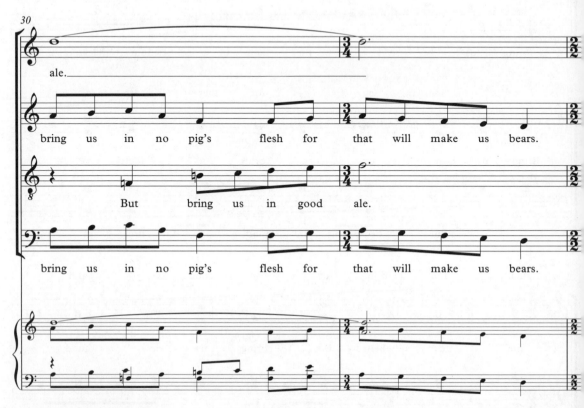

*Piano reduction for rehearsal only.

Bring us in no ca - pon's flesh for that is of - ten dear, Nor

Bring us in no ca - pon's flesh for that is of - ten dear, Nor

Bring us in no ca - pon's flesh for that is of - ten dear, Nor

Bring us in good ale, But bring us in good ale, But bring us in good

bring us in no duck's flesh for they slob - ber in the mere, But bring us in good ale.

bring us in no duck's flesh for they slob - ber in the mere, But bring us in good ale.

bring us in no duck's flesh for they slob - ber in the mere, But bring us in good ale.

ale, But bring us in good ale,_____ But bring us in good ale.

for Frank Sargent and the Highland Park High School Lads and Lassies, Dallas, Texas

4. Buffalo Gals

American traditional
arr. BOB CHILCOTT

5. Calme des nuits

Anonymous
tr. Olivia McCannon

CAMILLE SAINT-SAËNS

6. Chick, chick, chicken!

HOLT, McGHEE, and KING
arr. PETER GRITTON

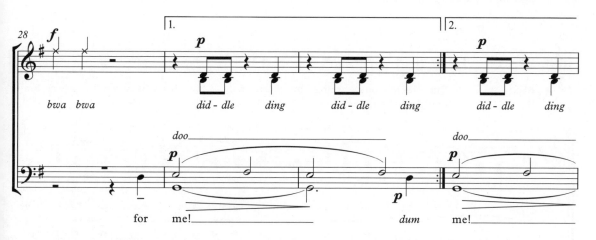

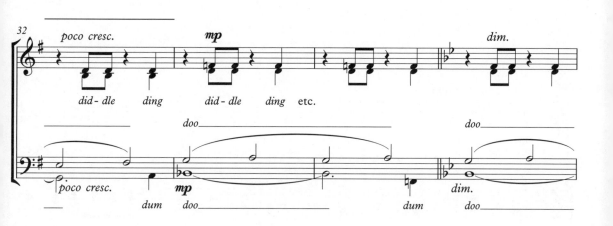

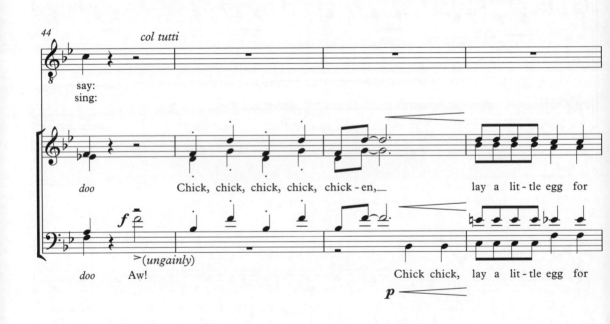

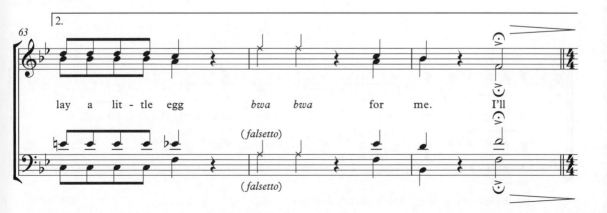

Slow, flexible barbershop tempo

lay you love this lit - tle lay,___ it's such a pret - ty
such a pret - ty,
such a pret - ty

molto rall.

so just to end, let's
thing,___ So just to fin - ish up this lay, let's all lay down and
pret - ty thing, So just to end this lay,
thing,___ So just to fin - ish up this lay,

Presto—fly the coop

sing:___ Oh! Chick, chick, chick, chick, chick - en,___
Woof, woof!

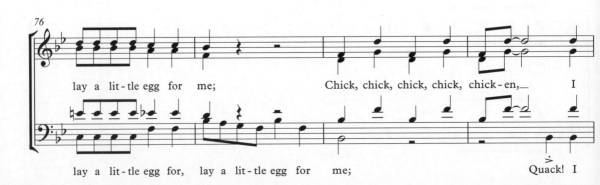

lay a lit - tle egg for me; Chick, chick, chick, chick, chick-en,___ I
lay a lit - tle egg for, lay a lit - tle egg for me; Quack! I

7. Counting Up My Toes

Anon.

DAVID CULLEN

Not slowly, with child-like simplicity

A-ny night that I can't sleep and have no time for count-ing sheep, I

know that I can al-ways doze if I start count-ing up my toes. I

know that when I get to ten my eyes will start to close, Those

rit. *faster*

ma-gic num-bers bring me slum-bers when I'm count-ing up my toes.

8. Country Gardens

English traditional
arr. PETER GRITTON

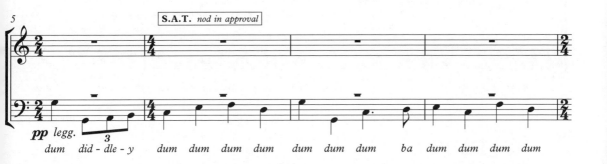

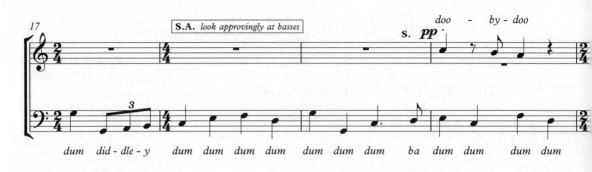

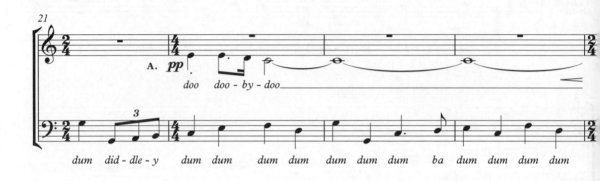

...lish coun - try...

Shh!

...lish coun - try...

dum dum dum dum   dum did - dle - y   dum dum dum dum   dum dum dum ba

Hmm! Hmm!

tra   la la la   la   la la la la la   la   la la la la

dum dum dum dum   dum did - dle - y   dum dum dum dum   dum dum dum ba

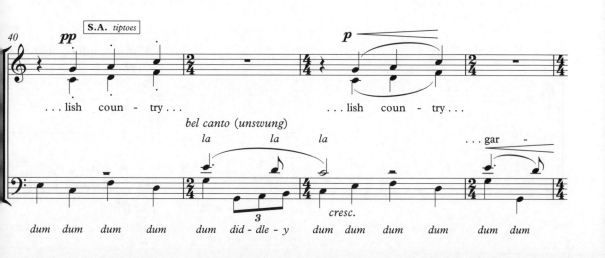

...lish coun - try...   ...lish coun - try...

bel canto (unswung)

la   la   la   ...gar -

dum dum dum dum   dum did - dle - y   dum dum dum dum   dum dum

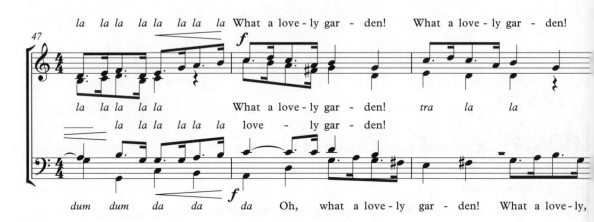

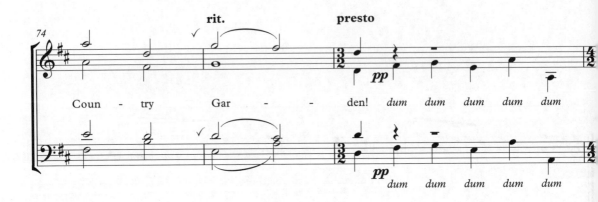

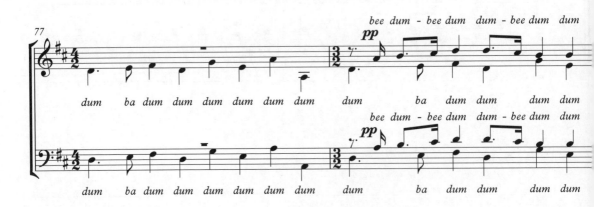

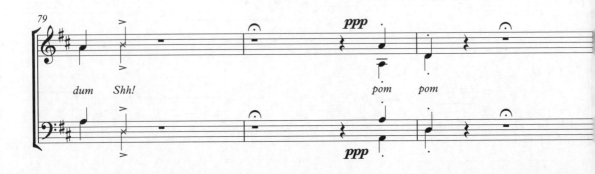

9. Dashing Away with the Smoothing Iron

English traditional
arr. JOHN RUTTER

looked   so nim-ble   starch-ing her lin - en O,   Dash -

looked   so nim-ble   starch-ing her lin - en O,   Dash -

nim - ble O   A - starch-ing of   her lin - en O,   Dash-ing a - way with the

looked   so nim-ble   starch-ing her lin - en O,   Dash -

- ing   a - way,   dash - ing a - way,   dash-ing a - way with the

- ing   a - way,   dash - ing a - way,   dash-ing a - way with the

smooth-ing iron,   Dash-ing a - way with the smooth - ing iron,   dash-ing a - way with the

- ing   a - way,   dash - ing a - way,   dash-ing a - way with the

Dash - ing a - way with the smooth - ing iron She stole my heart a - way.___ ah___

Dash - ing a - way with the smooth - ing iron She stole my heart a - way.___ ah___

5. 'Twas on a Fri - day

Dash - ing a - way with the smooth - ing iron She stole my heart a - way.___ ah___

Dash - ing a - way with the smooth - ing iron She stole my heart a - way. ah___

ah___

ah___

morn - ing And there I saw my dar - ling, She looked so neat and charm - ing In

ah___

ah___

dedicated to the King's Singers

10. Deconstructing Johann

DARYL RUNSWICK
(with thanks to J. S. BACH)

The original version is written a tone lower, thereby preserving Bach's keys.

most of a, most of a, most of a ra - ther fab - u - lous, fab - u - lous, fab - u - lous work.

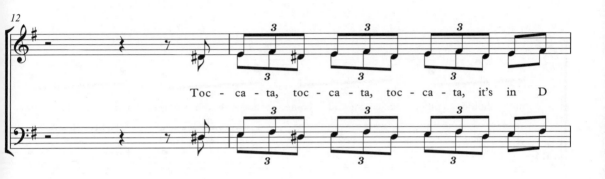

Toc - ca - ta, toc - ca - ta, toc - ca - ta, it's in D

mi - nor, D mi - nor, D mi - nor, but now I'm feel - ing, I'm feel - ing a bit of a burk.

I   can't think of, can't think of, can't think of, can't think of,

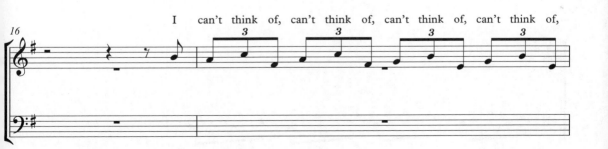

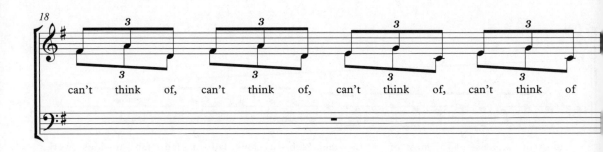

can't   think   of,   can't   think   of,   can't   think   of,   can't   think   of

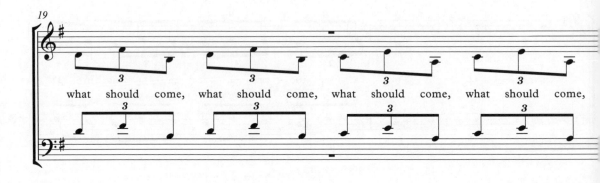

what   should   come,   what   should   come,   what   should   come,   what   should   come,

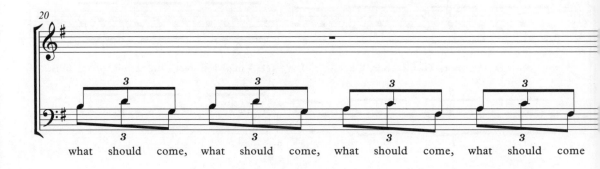

what   should   come,   what   should   come,   what   should   come,   what   should   come

af - ter   it,   af - ter   it,   af - ter   it,   af - ter   it . . .

*At this point a mobile phone goes off in one of the singers' pockets. The ring is the *Fugue in D Minor* that Bach is wanting inspiration for!

Choir Pantomime: You think it's a phone in the audience; then you realise that it's one of yours. The person with the phone answers it, hands it to 'Bach' and says: 'It's your agent!'. 'Bach' listens for a moment and says 'Aaaaaah!'.

to the choir of St Paul's Boys and Girls Schools, London

11. Dry Bones

Spiritual
arr. PETER GRITTON

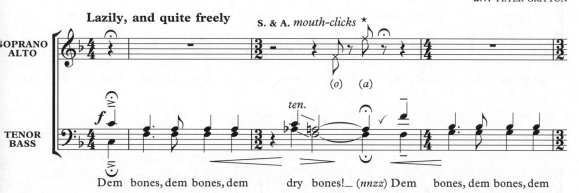

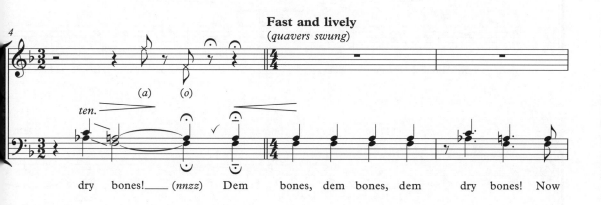

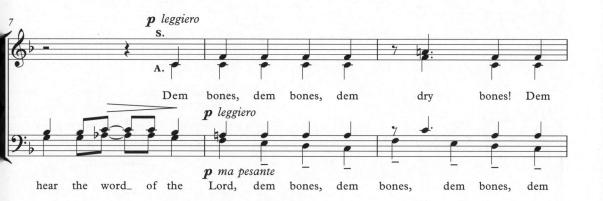

mouth-click: tongue leaves roof of mouth quickly, delivered with the given vowel.

© Oxford University Press 2004. Photocopying this copyright material is ILLEGAL.

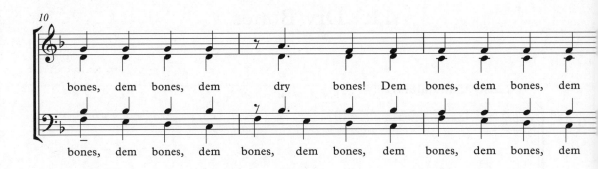

bones, dem bones, dem dry bones! Dem bones, dem bones, dem

bones, dem bones, dem bones, dem bones, dem bones, dem bones, dem

dry bones! Now hear the word of the Lord! E -

bones, dem bones, Now hear the word, Oh E - ze - ki - el

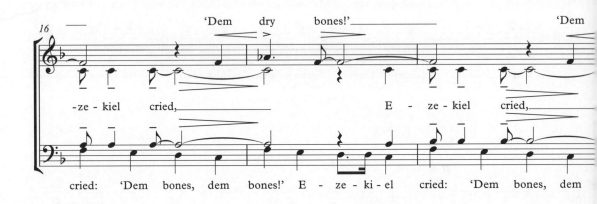

'Dem dry bones!' 'Dem

-ze - kiel cried, E - ze - kiel cried,

cried: 'Dem bones, dem bones!' E - ze - ki - el cried: 'Dem bones, dem

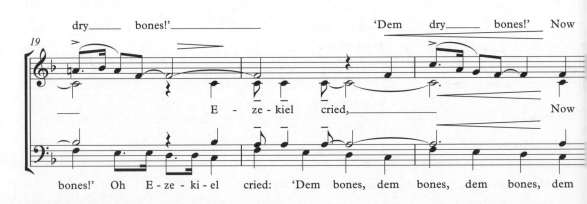

dry bones!' 'Dem dry bones!' Now

E - ze - kiel cried, Now

bones!' Oh E - ze - ki - el cried: 'Dem bones, dem bones, dem bones, dem

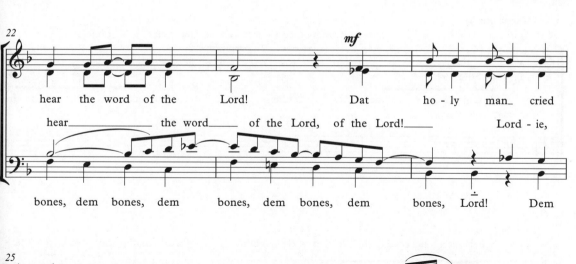

hear the word of the Lord! Dat ho - ly man_ cried
hear_____ the word_ of the Lord, of the Lord!_____ Lord - ie,
bones, dem bones, dem bones, dem bones, dem bones, Lord! Dem

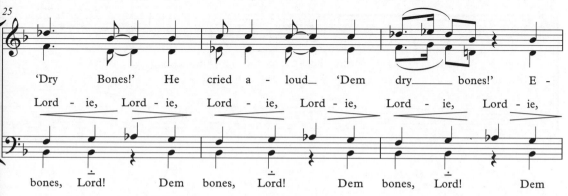

'Dry Bones!' He cried a - loud_ 'Dem dry_____ bones!' E -
Lord - ie, Lord - ie, Lord - ie, Lord - ie, Lord - ie, Lord - ie,
bones, Lord! Dem bones, Lord! Dem bones, Lord! Dem

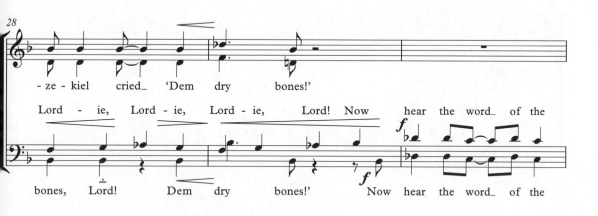

- ze - kiel cried_ 'Dem dry bones!'
Lord - ie, Lord - ie, Lord - ie, Lord! Now hear the word_ of the
bones, Lord! Dem dry bones!' Now hear the word_ of the

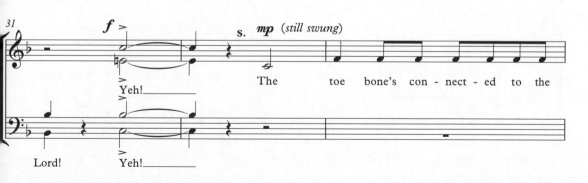

Yeh!_____ The toe bone's con - nect - ed to the
Lord! Yeh!_____

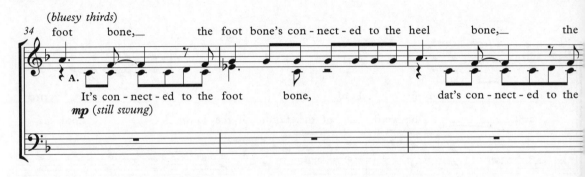

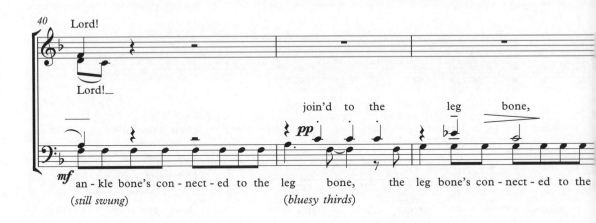

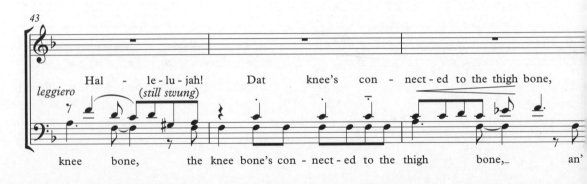

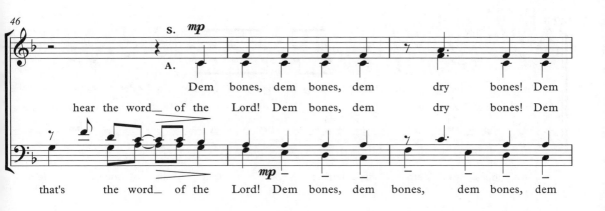

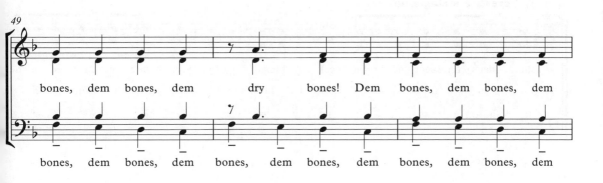

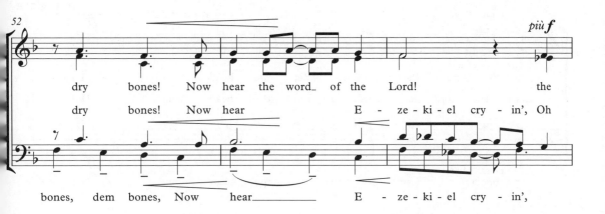

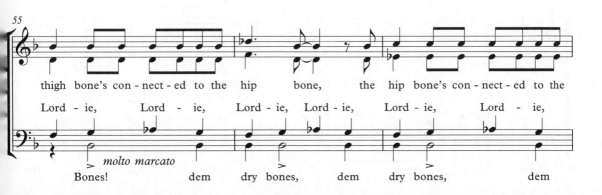

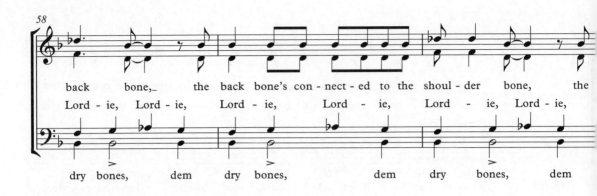

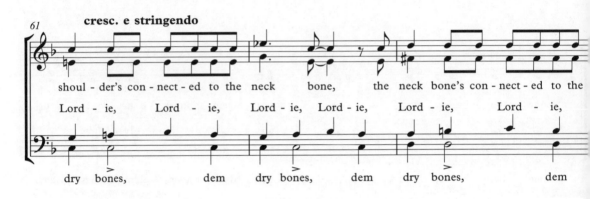

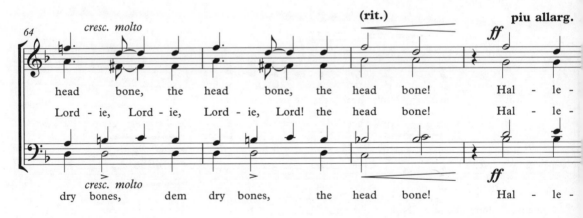

molto allarg.

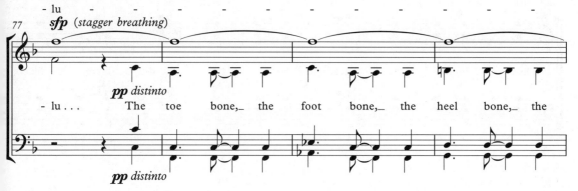

Presto

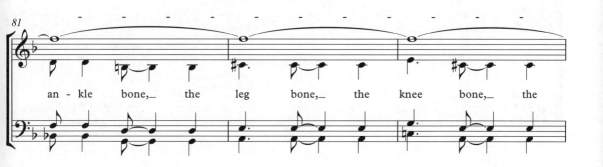

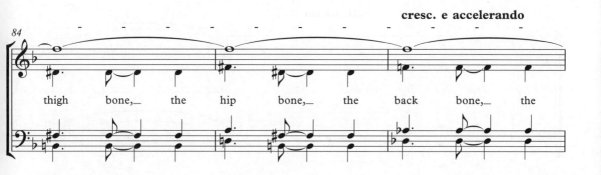

cresc. e accelerando

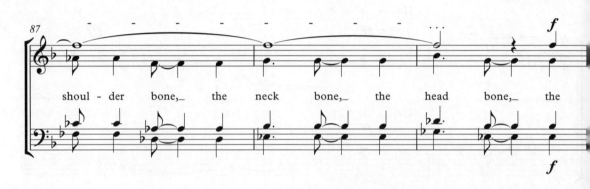

shoul - der bone,_ the neck bone,_ the head bone,_ the

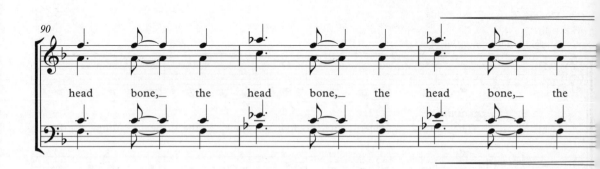

head bone,_ the head bone,_ the head bone,_ the

allargando al fine

head bone!_ Oh Lord!___

Oh my Lord - ie

rall. molto

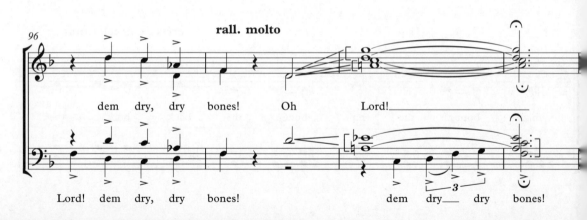

dem dry, dry bones! Oh Lord!___

Lord! dem dry, dry bones!   dem dry__ dry bones!

Commissioned by the Cantinovum choir of Jyväskylä, Finland

12. El Hambo

JAAKKO MÄNTYJÄRVI

Please note: the words above have no meaning; they are all nonsense sounds.

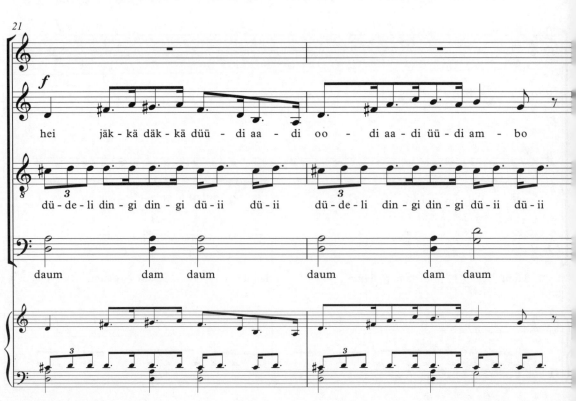

*The lower soprano part must be heard clearly. It may be advisable, for instance, to have S.2 and A.1 exchange parts in bars 31–8. This is meant to sound chaotic, by the way.

for Sheila Harrod and the Kentwood Choir

13. Ev'ry time I feel the Spirit

Spiritual
arr. BOB CHILCOTT

14. Good Hope

An African Blessing

Words from Ethiopia,
South Africa, and Nigeria

PETER GRITTON

♪ This symbol means mouth-click.
Translation for bars 1–16: 'God bless us, look after us; God bless Africa.'

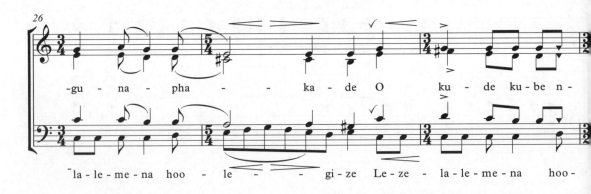

bars 17–29: 'For ever and ever.'

bars 31–42: 'We must not look back.'

15. Ill Wind

FLANDERS AND SWANN after MOZART

arr. PETER GRITTON

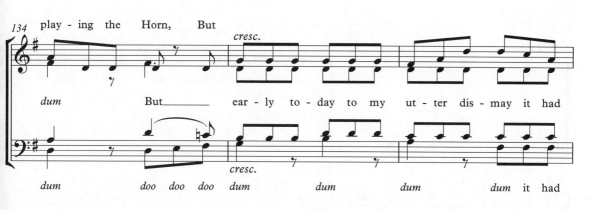

playing the Horn, But

dum   But   ear-ly to-day to my ut-ter dis-may it had

dum   doo doo doo dum   dum   dum   dum it had

to-tal-ly va-nished a-way.   ba ba ba ba ba ba ba ba ba ba ba ba ba ba ba

PIANO

ba ba

ba

ba ba ba ba ba ba ba ba ba ba ba ba   ba   ba   ba

157

-way,   they took it a-way,   they took it a-way,   they took it a-

neigh-bour's a-sleep in his bed.   I'll soon make him wish he were

-way,   they took it a-way,   they took it a-way,   they took it a-

neigh-bour's a-sleep in his bed.   I'll soon make him wish he were

160

-way.

dead.

ff

I'll take up the Tu-ba in-stead!   wah!   wah!

-way.

dead.

ff

ff

for Alan and Phyllis Frank

16. It was a lover and his lass

William Shakespeare

JOHN RUTTER

*A double bass part to accompany this piece is available on sale from Oxford University Press (ISBN 0 19 338026 9).
The piano part is primarily intended as a rehearsal aid, but may be played in performance. If possible, players should extemporize an appropriate keyboard part in jazz style. N.B. ♩♪ = ♩ ♪ always.

17. Jargon

WILLIAM BILLINGS

18. Mission: Impossible

LALO SCHIFRIN
arr. MARK WILLIAM

*(flute sound)

A breathy 'to-do-to' sound.

*A 'buh-duh-duh' or 'buh-dl-duh' (i.e. neutral vowels) sound, sung with closed mouth.

(muted trumpet sound)

19. Nachtlied
(*Evening Hymn*)

Petrus Herbert
tr. Emma Greengrass

MAX REGER

wir uns le-gen in seim Gleit und Se - gen, der Ruh zu pfle-
leads us with a bles-sing, to His King-dom to sleep so sound-

-gen. Treib, Herr, von uns fern die un-rei-nen Gei-ster, halt die Nacht-wach gern,
-ly. O Lord, keep us safe from all ev-il spi-rits; guard us lov-ing-ly

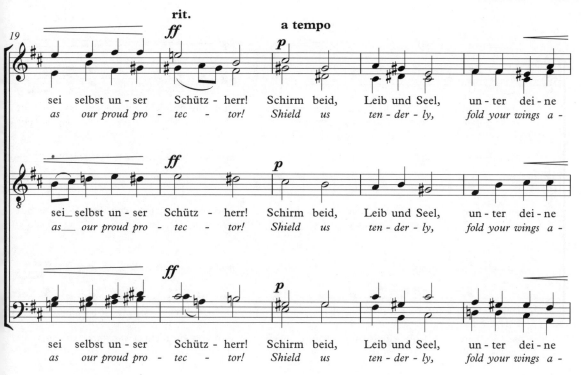

-dan - ken fröh - lich auf - wa - chen und von dir nicht wan - ken, lass uns mit
tran - quil; our wak - ing, joy - ful! By your side for ev - er, so shall our

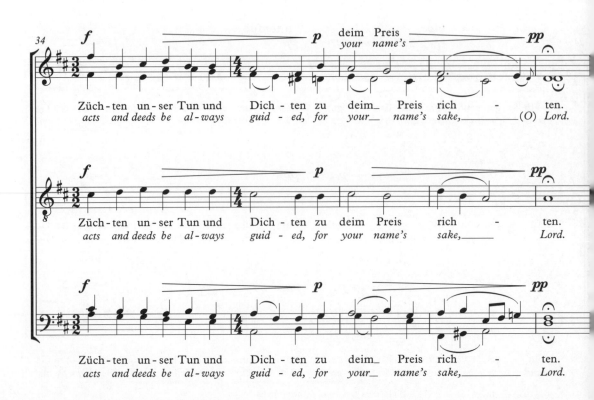

Züch - ten un - ser Tun und Dich - ten zu deim Preis rich - ten.
acts and deeds be al - ways guid - ed, for your name's sake,_____ (O) Lord.

20. Orpheus in the Underground

John Hudson

JACQUES OFFENBACH
arr. CANTABILE*

21. Parting Friends

North American traditional
arr. JOHN G. McCURRY

Simply *p*

Fare - well, my friends, I'm bound for Ca - naan, I'm trav'l - ling

through the wil - der - ness; Your com - pa - ny has been de - light - ful,

You, who doth leave my mind dis - tressed. I go a - way, be - hind to

leave you, Per - haps ne - ver to meet a - gain, But if we ne -

- ver have the plea - sure, I hope we'll meet on Ca - naan's land.

for the University of Richmond Choir, European tour 1971

22. Shenandoah

American traditional
arr. JAMES ERB

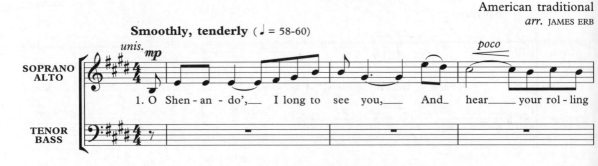

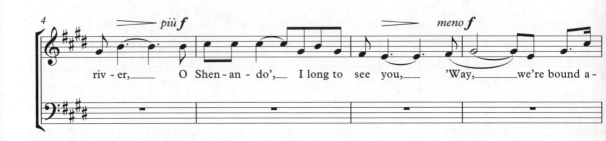

*Piano reduction for rehearsal only.

*alternative:

Shen - an -

23. Stranger in Paradise

WRIGHT and FORREST
after BORODIN
arr. PETER GRITTON

*Plus some tenors/baritones until bar 47.

poco a poco allargando al fine

Tenors/baritones *col tutti*.

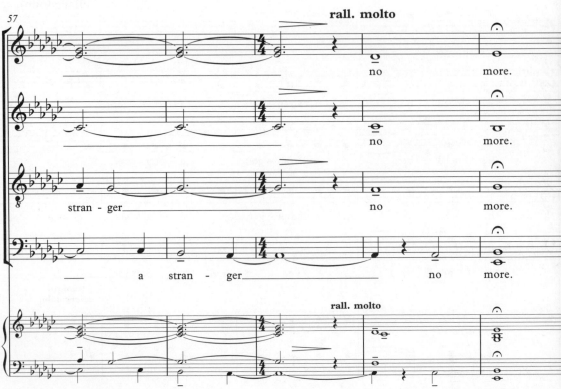

24. Take it from Figure 'O'

Ben Parry

W. A. MOZART
arr. BEN PARRY

rub - bish like the o - ther things we play it's a won - der I should

rub - bish like the o - ther things we play it's a won - der I should

cresc.

say that the au - di - ence will stay af - ter what they have to

cresc.

say that the au - di - ence will stay af - ter what they have to

cresc.

25. The Long Day Closes

Henry Chorley

ARTHUR SULLIVAN

*The small notes in the bass part are intended for use as *additional* notes, when the partsong is performed by a chorus.
From the collection *English Romantic Partsongs*, ed. Paul Hillier (ISBN 0-19-343650-7)

-dea-vour,   To count   the sounds of   mirth,_____   Now dumb   for ev - er.

Heed   not how   hope be-lieves   And fate dis-po - ses: Sha - dow is round the

eaves,   The   long day____   clo - ses;   The light - ed win - dows

The light - ed win - dows dim

dim   Are   fa - ding   slow - ly.   The fire   that was so trim   Now   quiv - ers____

Are fa - ding slow - ly.   The fire   that was so trim   Now   quiv - ers

low - ly,   quiv - ers low - ly.   Go   to the dream - less bed   Where grief   re-

-po-ses, Thy book of toil is read,— The long— day clo-ses Go—

Go to the dream-less bed Where grief re-po-ses; Thy book of toil is

— to the dream-less bed Where grief re-po-ses; Thy

Go to the dream-less bed where grief re-po-ses; Thy

Go to thy dream-less

thy book of toil is read,—

read,— thy book of toil is read,

Go to the

dim.
thy book of toil is read,—

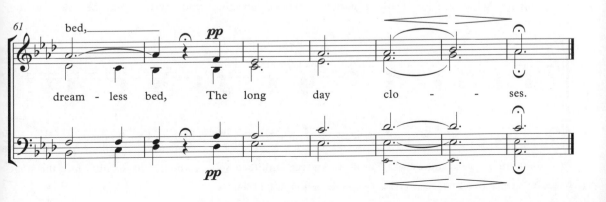

bed,— pp

dream-less bed, The long day clo - ses.

dim.
thy book of toil is read,—

pp

26. The tide rises, the tide falls

Henry Wadsworth Longfellow

HOWARD SKEMPTON

to Motley Croon

27. Three-minute Messiah

PETER GRITTON
(with thanks to
GEORGE FREDERICK HANDEL

The conductor continues
beating time in vain,
looking worried . . .

The conductor turns triumphantly and bows in the rests, carrying on bowing while the choir continues regardless.

28. 'Un'-Popular Song

Robin Barry

WILLIAM WALTON
arr. RODERICK WILLIAMS

*These interjections might be best as solos, from different people each time.

'Ba's' very nasal (like muted sheep.)

Pronounced 'dring-king'.

Rather than sounding precise, this should be delivered as a semi-drunken scoop within a legato phrase.

59

Ten se-conds left, to or-der a gin.

Soon as we're done, I'm get-ting them in.

61

... four three two one,   Chin,   chin!

... se'en six five four ...   Chin,   chin!

... ten nine eight se'en   Chin,   chin!

Count-ing down: ten ...   Chin,   chin!

*2nd tenor part could be allocated to 1st basses.

29. Vocalise

SERGEI RACHMANINOV
arr. PETER GRITTON

aw etc.
ah etc.

aw etc.
ah etc.

aw etc.
ah etc.

to Hans H. Rehberg and the Berlin Radio Choir

30. Wiegenlied

(*Lullaby*)

Verse 1: from *Des Knaben Wunderhorn*
Verse 2: Georg Scherer
tr. Emma Greengrass

JOHANNES BRAHMS
arr. ROBIN GRITTON

*It is preferred that some mezzos join the sopranos on the tune until bar 16.

Some baritones join tenors until bar 24.

früh,   wenn Gott will,   Wirst du   wie - der ge - weckt.   oo
God,   you   will wake,   Touch'd by   dawn's_ sweet   car - ess.

(**S.A.T.B**: '*oo*' gradually
opens out to '*ah*')